YEAR ONE

ELEMENTARY LATIN WORKBOOK

Published in the United States by Nyansa Classical Community
2416 S. Derbigny St.
New Orleans, LA 70125
nyansaclassicalcommunity.org

To order additional materials, please go to
www.nyansaclassicalcommunity.org

ISBN 978-1-967443-16-1 (Paperback)
ISBN 978-1-967443-17-8 (eBook)

Cover design by Laura Duffy
Book design by Sarah Scudder
Content developed by Dr. Angel Parham
Poems written by Rebecca Tellinghuisen

Printed in the United States of America

Credits

Stories Public Domain Aesop's Fables
English and Latin Poems Written by Rebecca Tellinghuisen
Formatting and Designed by Sarah Scudder
Edited by Sophia Scudder
Originally developed by Dr. Angel Adams Parham, Co-Founder and Executive
Director of Nyansa Classical Community

Acknowlegments

Thank you to the following organization for their support and funding:

Nyansa Classical Community

Founded by Dr. Angel Adams Parham, Nyansa Classical Community provides
classical, Christian curricula and programming designed to connect with and draw
students from diverse backgrounds into the beauty of classical literature and the
Great Conversation. For more information, please go to
nyansaclassicalcommunity.org.

Nyansa Materials

This workbook is intended to be used alongside our Year One Elementary Curricula.
This book should be purchased with Nyansa Year One Latin Teacher's Guide and
Year One Teacher's Guide.
To order additional materials please go to: www.nyansaclassicalcommunity.org

Resources

To access our Latin closing games, training videos, and other resources, scan the QR code below. For more training and information, you can buy our Year One Teacher's Guide online. You can also contact us at nyansa.assistant@gmail.com for access to our training materials.

Introduction

Nyansa's Latin curriculum is designed to provide an introduction to basic Latin vocabulary to students. This workbook should be used alongside our Year One Elementary Latin Teacher's Guide. Each lesson includes Latin vocabulary, a short story using fables, discussion, and games. The curriculum can be used over a four day period, however, the curriculum can be used to fit the schedule of your individual program.

The curriculum works best when students can review the vocabulary words each week. This workbook uses copywork, writing and drawing exercises, narration, poetry memorization, and vocabulary review to help students practice the Latin vocabulary weekly. The English language uses many Latin roots and parts of words. Gaining an understanding of these roots and parts of words will expand the vocabulary of your students for English. It will build up their language skills, reading skills, and communication.

Each week's activities will include the following:
- Reading a fable
- Copywork
- Narration
- Memorization
- Vocabulary Review

Note: Some weeks have vocabulary review activities included in this workbook. For the weeks without a workbook vocabulary review, please choose an activity/game featured in our Latin Teacher's Guide to review vocabulary. There are many to choose from.

Love: Caring for a person or thing very much and wishing good towards them.

Hate: Disliking a person or thing very much and wishing harm towards them.

The Dogs and the Fox

Illustrator: Harrison Weir, John Tenniel, Ernest Griset, et.al., public domain.

Some Dogs found the skin of a Lion and furiously began to tear it with their teeth. A Fox chanced to see them and laughed scornfully. "If that Lion had been alive," he said, "it would have been a very different story. He would have made you feel how much sharper his claws are than your teeth."

Copywork

Copy the vocabulary words below.

Vocabulary Bank:

Canēs – dog (canine)

Leonem/Leō – lion (Leo the constellation)

Vulpēs – fox

Verum – truth (verify)

Virtutem – courage (virtue)

Falsam – false

Victorēs – victorious (victor, victory)

Pugnāre – fight (pugnacious)

Copywork

Memorize

Memorize the poem below. See if you can memorize the poem in English and Latin.

Poem in English
The Dogs and the Fox

The dogs attacked the lion's skin,
but the fox knew the truth,
and he laughed at their false courage.
They were victorious that day,
only because the lion couldn't fight.

Moral: It is easy to feel strong when your enemy has no power.

Poem in Latin
Canes et Vulpis

Canēs pellem leōnis oppugnant,
sed vulpēs verum scit,
et virtutem falsam rīdet.
illo diē sunt victorēs,
solum quod leō pugnāre nōn potest.

Praeceptum: Facile est sentīre sē fortem ubi hostis potestātem nōn habet.

Narration

The Dogs and the Fox (Canes et Vulpis)

Write a narration of the story below. Retell the story using as much detail as possible. After writing the retelling of the myth, include the moral. Use the prompts below to start your writing.

The story goes. . . .

The moral is . . .

Illustrate

Draw your own illustration of today's fable. Include as many Latin vocabulary words as you can in your illustration.

Vocabulary Review

Match the Latin word with the English meaning.

Leonem/Leo	Victorious (victor, victory)
Falsam	Dog (Canine)
Virtutem	Fox
Canes	False
Victorēs	Fight (pugnacious)
Pugnāre	Lion (Leo the Constellation)
Vulpēs	Courage (Virtue)

LATIN WEEK TWO: VIRTUE and VICE

Compassion: Feeling sorry for those who are suffering and wanting to help.

Indifference: Ignoring the suffering or needs of others.

The Lion and the Mouse

Milo Winter 1919

It once happened that a hungry Lion woke to find a Mouse just under his paw. He caught the tiny creature, and was about to make a mouthful of him, when the little fellow looked up, and began to beg for his life.

In the most piteous tone, the Mouse said: "Do not eat me. I meant no harm coming so near you. If you would only spare my life now, O Lion, I would be sure to repay you!"

The Lion laughed scornfully at this, but it amused him so much that he lifted his paw and let his brave little prisoner go free.

It befell the great Lion, not long afterward, to be in as evil a case as had been the helpless Mouse. And it came about that his life was to be saved by the keeping of the promise he had ridiculed.

He was caught by some hunters, who bound him with a strong rope, while they went away to find means for killing him.

Hearing his loud groans, the Mouse came promptly to his rescue, and gnawed the great rope till the royal captive could set himself free.

"You laughed," the little Mouse said, "at the idea of my being able to be of service to you. You didn't think I could repay you. But you see it has come to pass that you are as grateful to me as I was once to you. The weak have their place in the world as truly as the strong."

Draw your own illustration of today's fable.

Copywork

Copy the vocabulary words below.

Rēx (rēg-) – king (regal)
Leō – lion (the constellation Leo
Mūris – mouse
Audit – hear (audio, auditorium)
Vēnātōrēs – hunters
Parvum – small, little
Animalia – animal, creature
Amīcus – friend (amicable)

Copywork

Memorize

Memorize the poem below. See if you can memorize the poem in English and Latin.

Poem in English
The Lion and the Mouse

King of the beasts, the lion laughed
when he heard the mouse's promise.
But when hunters caught him
and bound him tight,
the small creature was indeed his friend.

Moral: A kind deed will be remembered.

Poem in Latin
Leo et Mūs

Rēx bēstiārum, leō rīdet
ubi prōmissum mūris audit.
Sed ubi vēnātōrēs eum capiunt
et artē eum ligant,
parvum animal verē est amīcus.

Praeceptum: Factum benignum memoriā tenēbitur.

Narration

The Lion and the Mouse (Leo et Mūs)
Write a narration of the story below. Retell the story using as much detail as possible. After writing the retelling of the myth, include the moral. Use the prompts below to start your writing.
The story goes. . . .
The moral is . . .

Illustrate

Draw your own illustration of today's fable. Include as many Latin vocabulary words as you can in your illustration.

Vocabulary Review

Fill in the blank with the correct English meaning

Leo -_____

Mūris -_____

Parvum - _____

Rēx (rēg) - _____

Amīcus - _____

Multis -_____

Animalia – _____

Vēnātōrēs – _____

Audit - _____

LATIN WEEK THREE: VIRTUE and VICE

Forgiveness: Not holding someone else's bad actions against them.

Vengeance: Trying to make someone suffer because of their actions towards you.

The Donkey, the Fox, and the Lion

Milo Winter 1919

A Donkey and a Fox had become close comrades, and were constantly in each other's company. While the Donkey cropped a fresh bit of greens, the Fox would devour a chicken from the neighboring farmyard or a bit of cheese filched from the dairy. One day the pair unexpectedly met a Lion. The Donkey was very much frightened, but the Fox calmed his fears.

"I will talk to him," he said.

So the Fox walked boldly up to the Lion.

"Your highness," he said in an undertone, so the Donkey could not hear him, "I've got a fine scheme in my head. If you promise not to hurt me, I will lead that foolish creature yonder into a pit where he can't get out, and you can feast at your pleasure."

The Lion agreed and the Fox returned to the Donkey.

"I made him promise not to hurt us," said the Fox. "But come, I know a good place to hide till he is gone."

So the Fox led the Donkey into a deep pit. But when the Lion saw that the Donkey was his for the taking, he first struck down the traitor Fox.

Describe what happened first, next, last from today's story. Write it below.

Copywork

Copy the vocabulary words below.

Asinus – donkey (ass)
Vulpēs – fox
Amīcī – friends (amity)
Leō – lion (leonine)
Appāret – appear (apparition)
Servāre – save
Miserum – poor, wretched (miserable)
Dūcit (ducere) – leads (duct, conduct)
Esuriens – hungry
Prīmum – first (primary)

Copywork

Memorize

Memorize the poem below. See if you can memorize the poem in English and Latin.

Poem in English
The Donkey, the Fox, and the Lion

Donkey and fox were once friends,
then the lion appeared.
Fox wanted to save himself
and led the poor donkey into a pit.
But the lion, still hungry, took the betrayer first.

Moral: He who betrays a friend often falls into his own trap.

Poem in Latin
Asinus, Vulpis, et Leo

Ōlim asinus et vulpēs sunt amīcī,
tunc leō appāret.
Vulpēs sē servāre cupit
et in foveam asinum miserum dūcit.
Sed leō, etiam esuriens, prōditōrem prīmum capit.

Praeceptum: Quī amīcum prōdidit saepe in laqueum suum incidit.

Narration

The Donkey, the Fox, and the Lion (Asinus, Vulpis, et Leo)
Write a narration of the story below. Retell the story using as much detail as possible. After writing the retelling of the myth, include the moral. Use the prompts below to start your writing.
The story goes. . . .
The moral is . . .

Vocabulary Review

Match the Latin word with the English meaning.

Vulpēs   Fox

Asinus   Save

Appāret   First

Servāre   Donkey

Prīmum   Friends

Miserum   Leads

Amīcī   Appears

Dūcit (ducere)   Poor

Esuriens   Hungry

LATIN WEEK FOUR: VIRTUE and VICE

Kindness: Treating others with respect, gentleness, and compassion.

Cruelty: Hurting others on purpose.

The Old Lion

C. Whittingham (1814)

A Lion had grown very old. His teeth were worn away. His limbs could no longer bear him, and the King of Beasts was very pitiful indeed as he lay gasping on the ground, about to die.

Where now is his strength and his former graceful beauty?

Now a Boar spied him, and rushing at him, gored him with his yellow tusk. A Bull trampled him with his heavy hoofs. Even a contemptible Ass let fly his heels and brayed his insults in the face of the Lion.

Copywork

Copy the vocabulary words below.

Leō - lion
Fortis – strong (fortitude)
Pulcher – beautiful (pulchrify)
Vetus – old (veteran)
Cōnsūmere – eat (consume)
Aper – boar
Taurus – bull (the constellation Taurus)
Asinus – donkey
Timent – fear (timid)
Priorem – former (prior)

Copywork

Memorize

Memorize the poem below. See if you can memorize the poem in English and Latin.

Poem in English
The Old Lion

Once the lion had been beautiful and strong,
but he was old and could not eat or move.
The boar, bull, and ass feared him before,
But now, instead of running away,
they attacked and mocked the former king.

Moral: It is cruel to mock those who have fallen.

Poem in Latin
Leo Vetus

Ōlim leō erat pulcher et fortis,
sed nunc vetus, cōnsūmere aut movēre nōn potest.
Aper, taurus, et asinus antea eum timent,
sed nunc, nōn currunt.
Rēgem priorem oppugnant et dērīdent.

Praeceptum: Crūdēle est irrīdēre illōs quī cecidērunt.

Narration

The Old Lion (Leo Vetus)

Write a narration of the story below. Retell the story using as much detail as possible. After writing the retelling of the myth, include the moral. Use the prompts below to start your writing.

The story goes. . . .

The moral is . . .

Vocabulary Review

Look at the pictures and write the words in the correct place

Leo	Pulcher	Asinus	Vulpēs
Vetus	Aper	Cōnsūmere	Dormis
Amīcī	Tauraus	Timent	Rēx

LATIN WEEK FIVE: VIRTUE and VICE

Humility: Acknowledging your own flaws and recognizing the gifts of others.

Cruelty: Thinking you are much better than other people.

The Donkey and the Wolf

Milo Winter 1919

A Donkey was feeding in a pasture near a wood when he saw a Wolf lurking in the shadows along the hedge. He easily guessed what the Wolf had in mind, and thought of a plan to save himself. So he pretended he was lame, and began to hobble as if he was in pain.

When the Wolf came up, he asked the Donkey what had made him lame, and the Donkey replied that he had stepped on a sharp thorn.

"Please pull it out," he pleaded, groaning. "If you do not, it might stick in your throat when you eat me."

The Wolf saw the wisdom of the advice, for he wanted to enjoy his meal without any danger of choking. So the Donkey lifted up his foot and the Wolf began to search very closely and carefully for the thorn.

Just then the Donkey kicked out with all his might, tumbling the Wolf a dozen paces away. And while the Wolf was slowly getting to his feet, the Donkey galloped away in safety.

"Serves me right," growled the Wolf as he crept into the bushes. "I'm a butcher by trade, not a doctor."

Write a narration of today's story. Use as many details as possible.

Copywork

Copy the vocabulary words below.

Asinus – donkey
Lupus – wolf
Advenientem – coming (advent)
Videt – see (video)
Cōnsilium – plan (counsel, council)
Pedem – foot (pedestrian)
Īnspicit - inspects
Spīnam – thorn (spine)
Sentit – feels (sensation)
Ēvādit – gets away, escapes (evade)

Copywork

Memorize

Memorize the poem below. See if you can memorize the poem in English and Latin.

Poem in English
The Donkey and the Wolf

Donkey saw the wolf approaching
and made a plan: "I'll be lame."
When the wolf inspected donkey's foot,
he didn't find a thorn—but felt a kick!
And the donkey got away.

Moral: One who acts falsely often fails to recognize another liar.

Poem in Latin
Asinus et Lupus

Asinus lupum advenientem videt
et cōnsilium capit: "Claudus ero."
Ubi lupus pedem asinī īnspicit,
spīnam nōn invenit—sed calcem sentit!
Et asinus ēvādit.

Praeceptum: Quī falsē agit saepe alium mendācem nōn agnōscit.

Narration

The Donkey and the Wolf (Asinus et Lupus)
Write a narration of the story below. Retell the story using as much detail as possible. After writing the retelling of the myth, include the moral. Use the prompts below to start your writing.

The story goes. . . .

The moral is . . .

Vocabulary Review

```
W W C U N T T S N Q N V E G G I W
V Z F R B E E K P Y G R P N N H A
E Z U L T Q D D J D S P R I I O J
L M E T N T I C I P S N I R V N Y
F V V H G S V Q E V W Y W A O E Y
P E K M T Y P G D C T B W C L S O
D U A R F L J O G N I Z A M A T S
X D O D P H P R E M O V E T L F E
A N E G V A C I O U S F I G U U N
G S Y V W E T Q V T ρ N N G F T T
Q W I G O A N K A O I I L T T I I
Z A E N P L V I O M N E S A H D T
F J F L U K E R E S A X O J G A U
J C I S H S Q M U N M B Z R U V M
H V Y W S S R X N T O V U O E G
V R B P E D E M R A R E U V H W X
E M U I L I S N O C G G M Y T H V
```

ĪNSPICIT	ADVENIENTEM	PEDEM
ĒVĀDIT	SPINAM	ASINUS
CŌNSILIUM	SENTIT	VIDET
LUPUS		

LATIN WEEK SIX: VIRTUE and VICE

Wisdom: Knowing the right thing to do in every different situation.

Foolishness: Making bad decisions and ignoring good advice.

The Old Lion and the Fox

MILO WINTER 1919

An old Lion, whose teeth and claws were so worn that it was not so easy for him to get food as in his younger days, pretended that he was sick. He took care to let all his neighbors know about it, and then lay down in his cave to wait for visitors. And when they came to offer him their sympathy, he ate them up one by one.

The Fox came too, but he was very cautious about it. Standing at a safe distance from the cave, he inquired politely after the Lion's health. The Lion replied that he was very ill indeed, and asked the Fox to step in for a moment. But Master Fox very wisely stayed outside, thanking the Lion very kindly for the invitation.

"I should be glad to do as you ask," he added, "but I have noticed that there are many footprints leading into your cave and none coming out. Pray tell me, how do your visitors find their way out again?"

Write a narration of today's story. Use as many details as possible.

Copywork

Copy the vocabulary words below.

Leō – lion
Vetus – old (veteran)
Capere – catch, seize (capture)
Cavernam – cave, cavern
Manet – stays, remains (mansion)
Vīcīnēs – neighbors (vicinity)
Vīsitant – visit (visitation)
Vulpēs – fox
Vestīgia – steps, tracks (investigate, vestige)
Videt – sees (video)
Sapienter – wisely (homo sapiens)
Invītātiōnem – invitation

Copywork

Memorize

Memorize the poem below. See if you can memorize the poem in English and Latin.

Poem in English
The Old Lion and the Fox

An old lion could not catch food,
so he stayed in his cave, pretending to be sick.
Neighbors visited him, but they did not leave.
When the fox noticed tracks in one direction only,
he wisely refused the lion's invitation.

Moral: Sharp eyes will discover false words.

Poem in Latin
Leo et Vulpes

Leō vetus capere nōn potest,
ita in cavernam manet, fingens morbum.
Vīcīnēs eum vīsitant, sed nōn dēcēdunt.
Ubi vulpēs vestīgia solum in unā parte animadvertit,
invītātiōnem leōnis sapienter recūsat.

Praeceptum: Oculī ācrēs verba falsa inveniet.

Narration

The Old Lion and the Fox (Leo et Vulpes)
Write a narration of the story below. Retell the story using as much detail as possible. After writing the retelling of the myth, include the moral. Use the prompts below to start your writing.
The story goes. . . .
The moral is . . .

Vocabulary Review

Match the Latin word with the English meaning.

Manet	Catch
Vulpēs	Eat
Leo	Fox
Animalia	Old
Capere	Lion
Sapienter	See
Timent	Feared
Invītātiōnem	Animals
Vīcīnēs	Neighbors
Cōnsūmere	Invitation
Videt	Wisely
Vetus	Stay

LATIN WEEK SEVEN: VIRTUE and VICE

Justice: Giving to each person what they deserve.

Foolishness: Keeping from others what rightfully belongs to them.

The Wolf and the Lion

MILO WINTER 1919

A Wolf had stolen a Lamb and was carrying it off to his lair to eat it. But his plans were very much changed when he met a Lion, who, without making any excuses, took the Lamb away from him.

The Wolf made off to a safe distance, and then said in a much injured tone:

"You have no right to take my property like that!"

The Lion looked back, but as the Wolf was too far away to be taught a lesson without too much inconvenience, he said:

"Your property? Did you buy it, or did the Shepherd make you a gift of it? Pray tell me, how did you get it?"

Narrate the story back. Include as many details as you can remember. Think about how you would change the story. Now tell your new story. Draw a picture to illustrate the new story.

Copywork

Copy the vocabulary words below.

Lupus – wolf
Agnum – lamb
Aufert – carries away (ferry)
Dēsīderat – wants (desire)
Leō - lion
Murmurat – complains (murmur)
Dīcit (dicere) – says (dictate, dictionary)
Recordāre – recall (record)

Copywork

Memorize

Memorize the poem below. See if you can memorize the poem in English and Latin.

Poem in English
The Wolf and the Lion

A wolf snatched a lamb
and was carrying it away,
but the lion wanted it too.
When the wolf complained, the lion said,
"Recall—you were the thief first."

Moral: Do not cry when the thing you stole is stolen.

Poem in Latin
Lupus et Leo

Lupus agnum capit
et eum aufert,
sed leō eum dēsīderat quoque.
Ubi lupus murmurat, leō dīcit,
"Recordāre—tū est prīmus fūr."

Praeceptum: Nōlī lacrimāre ubi rēs quam abstulistī aufertur.

Narration

The Wolf and the Lion (Lupus et Leo)
Write a narration of the story below. Retell the story using as much detail as possible. After writing the retelling of the myth, include the moral. Use the prompts below to start your writing.
The story goes. . . .
The moral is . . .

Vocabulary Review

Match the Latin word with the English meaning.

Agnum	Wolf
Recordāre	Lamb
Dēsīderat	Lion
Leo	Recall
Lupus	Complains (murmur)
Dīcit (dicere)	Says, dictate
Murmurat	Wants

LATIN WEEK EIGHT: VIRTUE and VICE

Gratitude: Being thankful for all things and blessing others.

Jealousy: Hating others and wanting what they have for yourself.

The Hungry Wolf and the Well-Fed Dog

MILO WINTER 1919

There was once a Wolf who got very little to eat because the Dogs of the village were so wide awake and watchful. He was really nothing but skin and bones, and it made him very downhearted to think of it.

One night this Wolf happened to fall in with a fine fat House Dog who had wandered a little too far from home. The Wolf would gladly have eaten him then and there, but the House Dog looked strong enough to leave his marks should he try it. So the Wolf spoke very humbly to the Dog, complimenting him on his fine appearance.

"You can be as well-fed as I am if you want to," replied the Dog. "Leave the woods; there you live miserably. Why, you have to fight hard for every bite you get. Follow my example and you will get along beautifully."

"What must I do?" asked the Wolf.

"Hardly anything," answered the House Dog. "Chase people who carry canes, bark at beggars, and fawn on the people of the house. In return you will get tidbits of every kind, chicken bones, choice bits of meat, sugar, cake, and much more besides, not to speak of kind words and caresses."

The Wolf had such a beautiful vision of his coming happiness that he almost wept. But just then he noticed that the hair on the Dog's neck was and the skin was chafed.

"What is that on your neck?"

"Nothing at all," replied the Dog.

"What! Nothing!"

"Oh, just a trifle!"

"But please tell me."

"Perhaps you see the mark of the collar to which my chain is fastened."

"What! A chain!" cried the Wolf. "Don't you go wherever you please?"

"Not always! But what's the difference?" replied the Dog.

"All the difference in the world! I don't care a rap for your feasts and I wouldn't take all the tender young lambs in the world at that price." And away ran the Wolf to the woods.

Copywork

Copy the vocabulary words below.

Lupus – wolf
Canis – dog
Convenit – meets (convention)
Speciē – appearance (species)
Sententiam dīxit – commented (sentence)
Vitam - life (vital, vitamin)
Laudat – praises (laud)
Putat – thinks (computer)
Grandem – grand
Catēnā – chain
Audit – Hears (audio)
Libertas - liberty

Copywork

Memorize

Memorize the poem below. See if you can memorize the poem in English and Latin.

Poem in English
The Hungry Wolf and the Well-Fed Dog

A hungry wolf met a dog
and commented on his fine appearance.
The dog praised the life of a pet.
The wolf thought it was grand,
until he heard about the chain and collar.

Moral: It is better to be free than to eat a meal in chains.

Poem in Latin
Lupus et Canis

Lupus ēsuriens canem convenit
Et dē speciē bellā sententiam dīcit.
Canis vitam dēliciae laudat.
Lupus putat rem esse grandem,
dum dē catēnā et collāre audit.

Praeceptum: Melius est habēre libertātem quam edere cēnam in catēnīs.

Narration

The Hungry Wolf and the Well-fed Dog (Lupus et Canis)
Write a narration of the story below. Retell the story using as much detail as possible. After writing the retelling of the myth, include the moral. Use the prompts below to start your writing.
The story goes. . . .
The moral is . . .

Vocabulary Review

Fill in the English definition in the blank.

Videt -_____

Grandem - _____

Convenit - _____

Canis - _____

Putat - _____

Invitat -_____

Lupus -_____

Libertas - _____

Audit - _____

Vital - _____

Laudat - _____

LATIN WEEK NINE: VIRTUE and VICE

Self-discipline: Being able to do the right thing even when tempted to do something else

Indiscipline: Acting without considering the consequences.

The Fox and the Goat

MILO WINTER 1919

A Fox fell into a well, and though it was not very deep, he found that he could not get out again. After he had been in the well a long time, a thirsty Goat came by. The Goat thought the Fox had gone down to drink, and so he asked if the water was good.

"The finest in the whole country," said the crafty Fox, "jump in and try it. There is more than enough for both of us."

The thirsty Goat immediately jumped in and began to drink. The Fox just as quickly jumped on the Goat's back and leaped from the tip of the Goat's horns out of the well.

The foolish Goat now saw what a plight he had got into, and begged the Fox to help him out. But the Fox was already on his way to the woods.

"If you had as much sense as you have a beard, old fellow," he said as he ran, "you would have been more cautious about finding a way to get out again before you jumped in."

Narrate the story back. Include as many details as you can remember. The story goes. . . .
Think about how you would change the story. Now tell your new story. Draw a picture to illustrate the new story.

Copywork

Copy the vocabulary words below.

Vulpēs – fox
Dēcīdit – fell down (deciduous)
Puteum – well
Captus – trapped (capture)
Caprum – goat (constellation Capricorn)
Invītat – invites (invitation)
Intrā – enter
Bibe – drink (imbibe)
Aquam – water (aqua, aquarium)
Salit – jumps
Tergō – back
Fugit – escapes (fugitive)

Copywork

Memorize

Memorize the poem below. See if you can memorize the poem in English and Latin.

Poem in English
The Fox and the Goat

A fox fell down into a well and was trapped.
So he invited a thirsty goat:
"Enter and drink the finest water!"
But when the goat jumped in the well,
the fox escaped on the goat's back.

Moral: Watch out for dangers when promised a fine reward.

Poem in Latin
Vulpis et Capra

Vulpēs in puteum dēcidit et captus est.
Ita caprum sitiēns invītat:
"Intrā et bibe aquam bellissimam!"
Et ubi caper in puteum salit,
Vulpēs in tergō caprī fugit.

Praeceptum: Cavē perīcula ubi praemium bellum prōmitteris.

Narration

The Fox and the Goat (Vulpis et Capra)
Write a narration of the story below. Retell the story using as much detail as possible. After writing the retelling of the myth, include the moral. Use the prompts below to start your writing.
The story goes. . . .
The moral is . . .

LATIN WEEK TEN: VIRTUE and VICE

Heroism: Using your strength or knowledge to help and protect others.

Exploitation: When you use someone's weakness to hurt them.

The Fox and the Lion

MILO WINTER 1919

A little fox was out playing one day, when a Lion came roaring along.

"Dear me," said the Fox, as he hid behind a tree, "I never saw a Lion before. What a terrible creature! His voice makes me tremble."

The next time the Fox met the Lion he was not so much afraid, but he kept a safe distance and said to himself, "I wish he would not make such a noise!"

The third time they met, the Fox was not frightened at all. He ran up to the Lion, and said, "What are you roaring about?"

And the Lion was so taken by surprise that, without saying a word, he let the Fox walk away.

It would not be safe for little foxes always to follow the example of this one, but it is often true that what our fear makes seem like a lion in the way has no danger in it if we meet it bravely.

Write a narration of today's story. Use as many details as possible.

Copywork

Copy the vocabulary words below.

Vulpēs – fox
Iuvenis – young (juvenile)
Leōnem – lion
Videt – sees (video)
Arborem – tree (arboretum)
Cēlat – hides (conceal)
Provocat – challenges (provoke)
Faciem – face (facial)
Verbum – word (verb, verbal)
Dīcit – says (dictate, diction)

Copywork

Memorize

Memorize the poem below. See if you can memorize the poem in English and Latin.

Poem in English
The Fox and the Lion

When the young fox first saw the roaring lion,
he hid behind a tree.
Next time, he passed by unafraid.
The next time, he challenged the lion to his face.
And the lion? He didn't say a word.

Moral: One who is wise will not be disturbed by the unwise.

Poem in Latin
Vulpis et Leo

Ubi vulpēs iuvenis leōnem fremens prīmum videt,
post aborem sē cēlat.
Deinde impavidē praeterit.
Deinde ad faciem leōnem provocat.
Et leō? Ille verbum nōn dīcit.

Praeceptum: Quī est sapiēns ā imprūdentibus nōn erit perturbātus.

Narration

The Fox and the Lion (Vulpis et Leo)
Write a narration of the story below. Retell the story using as much detail as possible. After writing the retelling of the myth, include the moral. Use the prompts below to start your writing.
The story goes. . . .
The moral is . . .

Vocabulary Review

Look at the pictures and write the words in the correct place

Vulpis	Arborem	Bibe	Lupus
Aquam	Caprum	Salit	Leonem
Faciem	Canis	Puteum	Catēnā

73

LATIN WEEK ELEVEN: VIRTUE and VICE

Generosity: Giving whatever you have to others cheerfully.

Miserliness: Selfishly keeping everything you have for yourself.

The Bear, the Fox, and the Lion

MILO WINTER 1919

Just as a great Bear rushed to seize a stray kid, a Lion leaped from another direction upon the same prey. The two fought furiously for the prize until they had received so many wounds that both sank down unable to continue the battle.

Just then a Fox dashed up, and seizing the kid, made off with it as fast as he could go, while the Lion and the Bear looked on in helpless rage.

"How much better it would have been," they said, "to have shared in a friendly spirit."

Copywork

Copy the vocabulary words below.

Ursus – bear (constellation Ursa Major)
Leō - lion
Haedum – kid, young goat
Dēsīderant – want (desire)
Ēsurientēs – hungry
Pugnant – fight (pugnacious)
Fessissimī – very tired (fessī = tired)
Collābuntur – collapse
Spectant – watch (spectator)
Vulpēs – fox
Cēnam – dinner
Capit (Capere) – takes (capture)

Copywork

Memorize

Memorize the poem below. See if you can memorize the poem in English and Latin.

Poem in English
The Bear, the Lion, and the Fox

A bear and a lion both wanted a young goat,
because they both were hungry.
They fought and fought
until they were very tired and collapsed.
Then they watched as a fox took the meal.

Moral: Those with a shared goal ought to work together.

Poem in Latin
Ursus, Leo, et Vulpis

Ursus et leō uterque haedum dēsīderant,
quod uterque ēsurientēs sunt.
Illī pugnant et pugnant
dum sunt fessissimī et collābuntur.
Tum spectant ut vulpēs cēnam capit.

Praeceptum: Quī cum mēta commūnī simul labōrāre dēbent.

Narration

The Bear, the Lion, and the Fox (Ursus, Leo, et Vulpis)
Write a narration of the story below. Retell the story using as much detail as possible. After writing the retelling of the myth, include the moral. Use the prompts below to start your writing.
The story goes. . . .
The moral is . . .

Vocabulary Review

Fill in the Latin word for the definition in the blank.

Fox -_____

Bear -_____

Hungry - _____

Tired - _____

Want- _____

Collapse -_____

Lion – _____

Watch/See – _____

Takes - _____

Kid/ Young Goat - _____

Fight - _____

LATIN WEEK TWELVE: VIRTUE and VICE

Hospitality: Welcoming others into your home and looking to serve them.

Inhospitality: Being unwelcoming and rude to others in your home.

The Wolf and the Goat

MILO WINTER 1919

A Wolf saw a Goat feeding at the top of a steep precipice, where he could not reach her.

"My dear friend," said the Wolf, "be careful! I am afraid you will fall and break your neck. Do come down to the meadow, where the grass is fresh and green."

"Are you very hungry?" said the Goat. "And is it your dinner time? And would you like to eat me? I think I will not go down to the meadow today, thank you."

And she capered contentedly about on the edge of the rock, as safe from falling as she was from the greedy Wolf with his false care for her.

Create a comic strip below to illustrate today's story. What happened first, next, and last.

Copywork

Copy the vocabulary words below.

Lupus - wolf
Caprum - goat
Saxō – rock
Cōnspicit – spies, catches sight of (spectator)
Invītat – invites (invitation)
Herba – grass (herb)
Recēns – fresh (recent)
Viridis – green
Fallitur – is fooled (fallacy)
Locum – place (location)
Tūtum – safe
Relinquit – Leaves (relinquish)

Copywork

Memorize

Memorize the poem below. See if you can memorize the poem in English and Latin.

Poem in English
The Wolf and the Goat

A wolf spied a goat on a rock,
so he invited the goat into the meadow,
where there was fresh, green grass.
But the goat was not fooled
and did not leave his safe spot.

Moral: Do not listen to those who promise greener grass.

Poem in Latin
Lupus et Capra

Lupus caprum in saxō cōnspicit,
ita in pratum caprum invītat,
ubi est herba recēns et viridis.
Sed caper nōn fallitur
et locum tūtum nōn relinquit.

Praeceptum: Nōlī auscultāre quibus herbam viridiorem prōmittentibus.

Narration

The Wolf and the Goat (Lupus et Capra)
Write a narration of the story below. Retell the story using as much detail as possible. After writing the retelling of the myth, include the moral. Use the prompts below to start your writing.
The story goes. . . .
The moral is . . .

_____

_____

_____

_____

_____

_____

_____

_____

_____

_____

_____

_____

_____

_____

_____

_____

_____

_____

Vocabulary Review

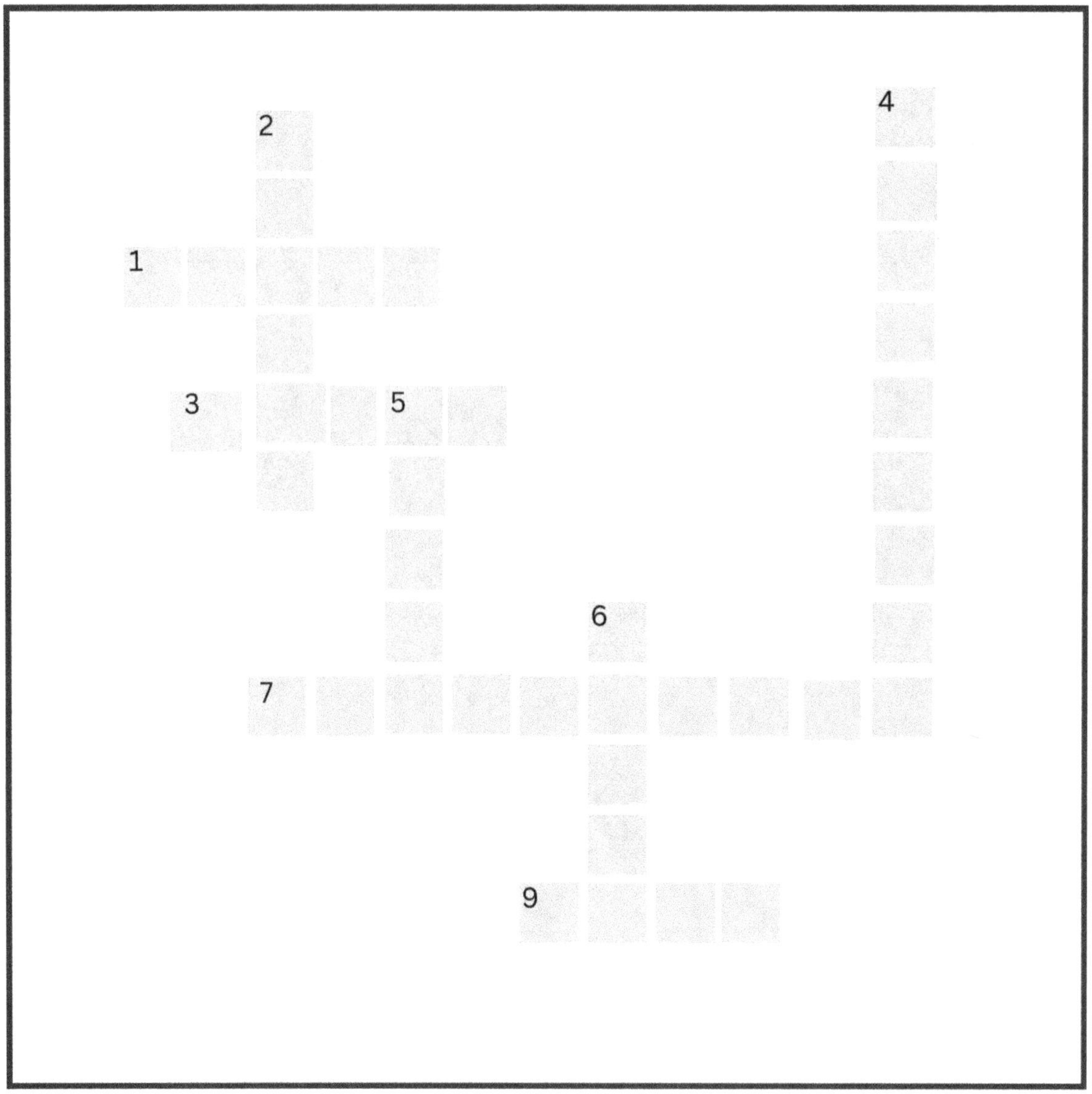

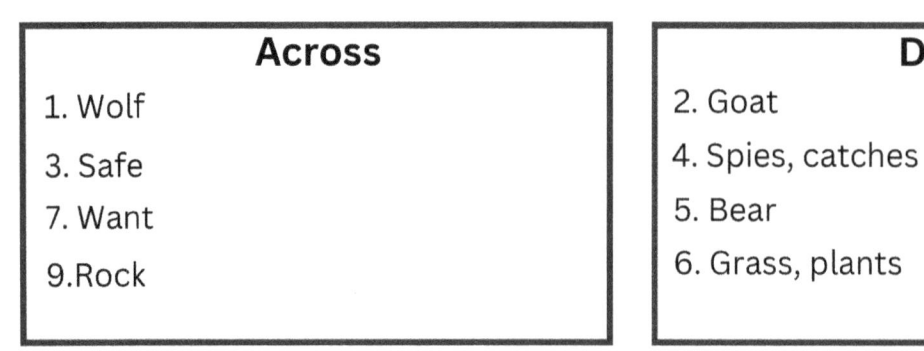

LATIN WEEK THIRTEEN: VIRTUE and VICE

Industriousness: Working hard and well at whatever you have to do.

Laziness: Doing work slowly adn badly or refusing to work at all.

The Cat and the Fox

MILO WINTER 1919

Once a Cat and a Fox were traveling together. As they went along, picking up provisions on the way—a stray mouse here, a fat chicken there—they began an argument to while away the time between bites. And, as usually happens when comrades argue, the talk began to get personal.

"You think you are extremely clever, don't you?" said the Fox. "Do you pretend to know more than I? Why, I know a whole sackful of tricks!"

"Well," retorted the Cat, "I admit I know one trick only, but that one, let me tell you, is worth a thousand of yours!"

Copywork

Copy the vocabulary words below.

Viā – road, way (viaduct)
Fēlēs – cat (feline)
Vulpēs – fox
Dolus (dolīs) – trick(s)
Canēs – dogs (canine)
Vēnātōris - hunter
Ūnus – one (uni-)
Vītam – life (vitality)
Servat – saves
Sequī – to follow (sequence)
Cōnsilium – idea (council)
Optimum – best (optimal)

Copywork

Memorize

Memorize the poem below. See if you can memorize the poem in English and Latin.

Poem in English
The Cat and the Fox

While on the road, a cat and a fox
argued about cleverness and tricks.
When the hunter's dogs approached,
the cat's one trick saved his life,
but the fox didn't know the best idea.

Moral: Too many good ideas can make you indecisive.

Poem in Latin
Feles et Vulpis

Dum in viā, fēlēs et vulpēs
dē calliditāte et dolīs disputant.
Ubi canēs vēnātōris appropinquant,
ūnus dolus fēlis vītam servat,
sed vulpēs cōnsilium optimum nēscit.

Praeceptum: Plūrima cōnsilia bona facere possunt tē dubius.

Narration

The Cat and the Fox (Feles et Vulpis)
Write a narration of the story below. Retell the story using as much detail as possible. After writing the retelling of the myth, include the moral. Use the prompts below to start your writing.
The story goes. . . .
The moral is . . .

Vocabulary Review

Match the Latin word with the English meaning.

Consilium	Dogs
Feles	One
Sequi	Cat
Dolus	Fox
Unus	Best
Canes	Saves
Venatoris	Tree
Servat	Plan
Vulpis	Better
Vitam	Tricks
Optimum	Life
Arborem	To Follow
	Hunter

LATIN WEEK FOURTEEN: VIRTUE and VICE

Contentment: Being happy with what you have.

Envy: Wanting what others have so much that you wish them harm.

The Rooster, the Dog, and the Fox

MILO WINTER 1919

A Dog and a Rooster, who were the best of friends, wished very much to see something of the world. So they decided to leave the farmyard and to set out into the world along the road that led to the woods. The two comrades traveled along in the very best of spirits and without meeting any adventure to speak of.

At nightfall the Rooster, looking for a place to roost, as was his custom, spied nearby a hollow tree that he thought would do very nicely for a night's lodging. The Dog could creep inside and the Rooster would fly up on one of the branches. So said, so done, and both slept very comfortably.

With the first glimmer of dawn, the Rooster awoke. For the moment he forgot just where he was. He thought he was still in the farmyard where it had been his duty to arouse the household at daybreak. So standing on tip-toes he flapped his wings and crowed lustily. But instead of awakening the farmer, he awakened a Fox not far off in the woods. The Fox immediately had rosy visions of a very delicious breakfast. Hurrying to the tree where the bird was roosting, he said very politely:

"A hearty welcome to our woods, honored sir. I cannot tell you how glad I am to see you here. I am quite sure we shall become the closest of friends."

"I feel highly flattered, kind sir," replied the Rooster slyly. "If you will please go around to the door of my house at the foot of the tree, my porter will let you in."

The hungry but unsuspecting Fox, went around the tree as he was told, and in a twinkling the Dog had seized him.

Copywork

Copy the vocabulary words below.

Canis – dog (canine)
Gallus – rooster
Arbore – tree (arbor, arboretum)
Vulpēs - fox
Dormiunt – sleep (dormitory)
Vulpem – fox
Proximum – nearby (proximal)
Excitat – awake (excite)
Salūtiōnem – welcome (salutation)
Accipit– receives (accept)
Iānuam – door (January)
Convenit – meet (convene)

Copywork

Memorize

Memorize the poem below. See if you can memorize the poem in English and Latin.

Poem in English
The Rooster, the Dog, and the Fox

A dog and a rooster slept in a tree one night.
At dawn, the rooster crowed as usual
and awoke a nearby fox.
The fox received a welcome from the rooster,
but at the door he met a hungry dog.

Moral: Those who flatter falsely will be fooled by the flattery of others.

Poem in Latin
Gallus, Canis, et Vulpis

Quādem nocte canis et gallus in arbore dormiunt.
Primā luce, gallus ut solet canit
et vulpem proximum excitat.
Vulpēs ā gallō salūtiōnem accipit,
sed apud iānuam canem ēsuriens convenit.

Praeceptum: Quī falsē blandiuntur ā blanditiā aliŏrum fallentur.

Narration

The Rooster, the Dog, and the Fox (Gallus, Canis, et Vulpis)
Write a narration of the story below. Retell the story using as much detail
as possible. After writing the retelling of the myth, include the moral. Use
the prompts below to start your writing.
The story goes. . . .
The moral is . . .

LATIN WEEK FIFTEEN: VIRTUE and VICE

Trustworthiness: Being honest and keeping your word.

Untrustworthiness: Telling lies, acting sneakily, or breaking promises.

The Wolf and the Young Goat

MILO WINTER 1919

Mother Goat was going to market one morning to get provisions for her household, which consisted of but one little Kid and herself.

"Take good care of the house, my son," she said to the Kid, as she carefully latched the door. "Do not let anyone in, unless he gives you this password:

"Down with the Wolf and all his race!'"

Strangely enough, a Wolf was lurking nearby and heard what the Goat had said. So, as soon as Mother Goat was out of sight, up he trotted to the door and knocked.

"Down with the Wolf and all his race," said the Wolf softly.

It was the right password, but when the Kid peeped through a crack in the door and saw the shadowy figure outside, he did not feel at all easy.

"Show me a white paw," he said, "or I won't let you in."

A white paw, of course, is a feature few Wolves can show, and so Master Wolf had to go away as hungry as he had come.

"You can never be too sure," said the Kid, when he saw the Wolf making off to the woods.

Copywork

Copy the vocabulary words below.

Mater – mother (maternal)
Capra – capra (constellation Capricorn)
Domō (domus) – house (domicile)
Ambulāvit – walked (ambulance)
Haedum – kid, young goat
Monet – warns (admonish)
Hostēs – enemies (hostile)
Lupus – wolf
Temptat – tries (tempt)
Cautus – cautious
Signum – sign (signify)
Petit – asks for
Pedem – paw, foot (pedestrian)
Dēmōnstrāre – show (demonstration)

Copywork

Memorize

Memorize the poem below. See if you can memorize the poem in English and Latin.

Poem in English
The Wolf and the Young Goat

Before the mother goat walked out of the house,
she warned her kid about enemies.
So when a wolf tried to give the password,
the cautious kid asked for a sign.
But the wolf could not show a white paw.

Moral: Better to be safe than sorry.

Poem in Latin
Lupus et Haedus

Anteā mater capra ē domō ambulat,
illa haedum dē hostēs monet.
Ita ubi lupus tesseram temptat dare,
haedus cautus signum petit.
Sed lupus pedem album dēmōnstrāre nōn potest.

Praeceptum: Melius est tuērī quam paenitēre.

Narration

The Wolf and the Young Goat (Lupus et Haedus)
Write a narration of the story below. Retell the story using as much detail as possible. After writing the retelling of the myth, include the moral. Use the prompts below to start your writing.
The story goes. . . .
The moral is . . .

LATIN WEEK SIXTEEN: VIRTUE and VICE

Gentleness: Being tender and kind with your actions and words.

Harshness: Treating others with cruelty and severity.

The Lion and the Donkey

MILO WINTER 1919

One day as the Lion walked proudly down a forest aisle, and the animals respectfully made way for him, a Donkey brayed a scornful remark as he passed.

The Lion felt a flash of anger. But when he turned his head and saw who had spoken, he walked quietly on. He would not honor the fool with even so much as a stroke of his claws.

Copywork

Copy the vocabulary words below.

Omnia – all (omni-)
Animālia – animals
Viam – way, path (viaduct)
Magnō – great (magnitude)
Faciunt – make (factory)
Leōnī – lion
Asinus – donkey
Exclāmat – yells, shouted (exclamation)
Vertit – turns
Videt – sees (video)
Locō – place (location)
Dēscendit - stoops, goes down (descend)

Copywork

Memorize

Memorize the poem below. See if you can memorize the poem in English and Latin.

Poem in English
The Lion and the Donkey

All the animals made a way
for the great and powerful lion.
But the donkey yelled out an insult.
The lion turned and saw the heckler,
but he did not stoop to the fool's level.

Moral: Do not repay insult with insult.

Poem in Latin
Leo et Asinus

Omnia animālia viam faciunt
magnō et validō leōnī.
Sed asinus contumēliam exclāmat.
Leō vertit et convīciātōrem videt,
sed locō tenus stultī nōn dēscendit.

Praeceptum: Nōlī reddere contumēliam contumēliā.

Narration

The Lion and the Donkey (Leo et Asinus)
Write a narration of the story below. Retell the story using as much detail as possible. After writing the retelling of the myth, include the moral. Use the prompts below to start your writing.
The story goes. . . .
The moral is . . .

Vocabulary Review

Fill in the Latin or English word in the blank.

All – _____

Lion – _____

Turns – _____

Place – _____

Donkey – _____

Animals – _____

Way, Path – _____

Great – _____

Stoops, Goes down – _____

LATIN WEEK SEVENTEEN: VIRTUE and VICE

Honesty: Telling the truth.

Dishonesty: Hiding the truth.

The Cat and the Birds

1905 Conde

A Cat was growing very thin. As you have guessed, he did not get enough to eat. One day he heard that some Birds in the neighborhood were ailing and needed a doctor. So he put on a pair of spectacles, and with a leather box in his hand, knocked at the door of the Bird's home.

The Birds peeped out, and Dr. Cat, with much solicitude, asked how they were. He would be very happy to give them some medicine.

"Tweet, tweet," laughed the Birds. "Very smart, aren't you? We are very well, thank you, and more so, if you only keep away from here."

Write a narration of today's story. Use as many details as possible.

Copywork

Copy the vocabulary words below.

Fēlēs – cat (feline)
Avibus – birds (aviary)
Audit – hears (audio)
Medicum – doctor (medic)
Medicāmentum – medicine, medication
Vident – see (video)
Rīdent – laugh
Invītant – invite (invitation)

Copywork

Memorize

Memorize the poem below. See if you can memorize the poem in English and Latin.

Poem in English
The Cat and the Birds

A hungry cat heard there were sick birds,
so he disguised himself as a doctor.
The cat offered the birds medicine,
but they saw him and laughed
and did not invite him inside.

Moral: Do not trust a person who takes advantage of the vulnerable.

Poem in Latin
Feles et Avis

Fēlēs ēsuriens dē avibus aegrīs audit,
ita sē medicum dissimulat.
Fēlēs medicāmentum avibus offert,
sed eum vident et rīdent
et eum intus nōn invītant.

Praeceptum: Nōlī crēdere hominī quī vulnerābilibus abūtitur.

Narration

The Cat and the Birds (Feles et Aves)
Write a narration of the story below. Retell the story using as much detail as possible. After writing the retelling of the myth, include the moral. Use the prompts below to start your writing.
The story goes. . . .
The moral is . . .

LATIN WEEK EIGHTEEN: VIRTUE and VICE

Fortitude: Being tender and kind with your actions and words.

Faint-heartedness: Treating others with cruelty and severity.

The Donkey in a Lion's Skin

MILO WINTER 1919

A Donkey once put on a Lion's skin which some hunters had spread out to dry. It did not fit the Donkey very well, but he found that in it he could frighten all the timid, foolish little animals, so he amused himself by chasing them about.

By and by he met a Fox, and tried to frighten him by roaring.

"My dear Donkey," said the wise Fox, "you are braying, and not roaring. I might, perhaps, have been frightened by your looks, if you had not tried to roar; but I know your voice too well to mistake you for a Lion."

Create a comic strip below to illustrate today's story. What happened first, next, and last.

Copywork

Copy the vocabulary words below.

Asinus – donkey
Pelle – skin (pelt)
Leōnis – lion (constellation Leo)
Parva – small
Animālia – animals
Terret – scares (terrify)
Vulpem – fox
Fallere – fool, trick, deceive (fallacy)
Vōx (voc-) – voice (vocal)
Speciem – appearance (species)
Adaequat – matches, equals
Fremit – roars

Copywork

Memorize

Memorize the poem below. See if you can memorize the poem in English and Latin.

Poem in English
A Donkey in a Lion's Skin

A donkey dressed in a lion's skin,
and he scared the little animals.
But he could not fool the fox
because his voice did not match his appearance.
A donkey does not roar like a lion.

Moral: Listen for the truth, because appearances often deceive.

Poem in Latin
Asinus in Belle Leonis

Asinus in pelle leōnis sē induit,
et parva animālia terret.
Sed vulpem fallere nōn potest
quod vōx speciem nōn adaequat.
Asinus nōn fremit sicut leō.

Praeceptum: Ausculta vēritātem, quod speciēs saepe dēcipit.

Narration

The Donkey in a Lion's Skin (Asinus in belle leonis)
Write a narration of the story below. Retell the story using as much detail as possible. After writing the retelling of the myth, include the moral. Use the prompts below to start your writing.
The story goes. . . .
The moral is . . .

LATIN WEEK NINETEEN: VIRTUE and VICE

Courage: Doing the right thing even when it's scary.

Cowardice: Letting fear control your actions.

The Cat and the Mice

Gustave Doré's illustration of La Fontaine's fable, c. 1868

Some little Mice, who lived in the walls of a house, met together one night, to talk of the wicked Cat and to consider what could be done to get rid of her. The head Mice were Brown-back, Gray-ear, and White-whisker.

"There is no comfort in the house," said Brown-back. "If I but step into the pantry to pick up a few crumbs, down comes the Cat, and I have hardly time to run to my nest again."

"What can we do?" asked Gray-ear. "Shall we all run at her at once and bite her, and frighten her away?"

"No," said White-whisker; "she is so bold we could not frighten her. I have thought of something better than that. Let us hang a bell around her neck. Then, if she moves, the bell will ring, and we shall hear it, and have time to run away."

"O yes! yes!" cried all the Mice. "That is a capital idea. We will bell the Cat! Hurrah! hurrah! No more fear of the Cat!" and they danced in glee.

When their glee had subsided a little, Brown-back asked, "But who will hang the bell around her neck?"
No one answered. "Will you?" he asked of White-whisker.

"I don't think I can," replied White-whisker; "I am lame, you know. It needs someone who can move quickly."

"Will you, Gray-ear?" said Brown-back.

"Excuse me," answered Gray-ear; "I have not been well since that time when I was almost caught in the trap."

"Who will bell the Cat, then?" said Brown-back. "If it is to be done, someone must do it."

Not a sound was heard, and one by one the little Mice stole away to their holes, no better off than they were before.

Copywork

Copy the vocabulary words below.

Mūrēs – mice
Cōnsilium – plan (counsel)
Pōnāmus (pos-) put (position)
Tintinnābulum - small bell (tinnitus)
Fēle – cat (feline)
Tūtī – safe
Nēmō – no one
Facere (faciō) – do, make (facilitate)
Nihil – nothing (*ex nihilo*)
Mūtat – changes (mutate)

Copywork

Memorize

Memorize the poem below. See if you can memorize the poem in English and Latin.

Poem in English
The Cat and the Mice

The mice had a plan:
"Let's put a bell on the cat,
so we will be safe!"
But no one wanted to do it,
and so nothing changed.

Moral: A bold plan seems good, but the deed itself is another matter.

Poem in Latin
Feles et Mures

Mūrēs cōnsilium capiunt:
"Pōnāmus tintinnābulum in fēle
ita tūtī erimus!"
Sed nēmō rem facere vult,
itaque nihil mūtat.

Praeceptum: Cōnsilium audax vidētur bonum, factum ipsum est aliam rem.

Narration

The Cat and the Mice (Feles et Mures)
Write a narration of the story below. Retell the story using as much detail as possible. After writing the retelling of the myth, include the moral. Use the prompts below to start your writing.
The story goes. . . .
The moral is . . .

Joy: Enthusiastically enjoying your blessings.

Despair: Letting fear control your actions.

The Donkey and the Dog

Milo Winter 1919

There was once a Donkey whose Master also owned a Lap Dog. This Dog was a favorite and received many a pat and kind words from his Master, as well as choice bits from his plate. Every day the Dog would run to meet the Master, frisking playfully about and leaping up to lick his hands and face.

All this the Donkey saw with much discontent. Though he was well fed, he had much work to do; besides, the Master hardly ever took any notice of him.

Now the jealous Donkey got it into his silly head that all he had to do to win his Master's favor was to act like the Dog. So one day he left his stable and clattered eagerly into the house.

Finding his Master seated at the dinner table, he kicked up his heels and, with a loud bray, pranced giddily around the table, upsetting it as he did so. Then he planted his forefeet on his Master's knees and rolled out his tongue to lick the Master's face, as he had seen the Dog do. But his weight upset the chair, and Donkey and the man rolled over together in the pile of broken dishes from the table.

The Master was much alarmed at the strange behavior of the Donkey, and calling for help, soon attracted the attention of the servants. When they saw the danger the Master was in from the clumsy beast, they set upon the Donkey and drove him with kicks and blows back to the stable. There they left him to mourn the foolishness that had brought him nothing but a sound beating.

Copywork

Copy the vocabulary words below.

Asinus – donkey
Canī (canis) – dog (canine)
Dominī – master (dominion)
Domum – house (domicile, domestic)
Intrat – enters
Agere – act, do, carry on
Magnās – great, large (magnificent)
Turbās – mess, chaos (turbulent)
Servī – servants
Pūniunt – punish (punitive)

Copywork

Memorize

Memorize the poem below. See if you can memorize the poem in English and Latin.

Poem in English
The Donkey and the Dog

A donkey envied his master's dog,
so he entered the house
and started to behave like a dog.
But he made a great mess,
and the master's servants punished him.

Moral: Discontent only leads to greater trouble.

Poem in Latin
Asinus et Canis

Asinus canī dominī invīdet,
ita domum intrat
et incipit se gerere sicut canis.
Sed magnās turbās concit.
et servī dominī eum pūniunt.

Praeceptum: Offēnsiōnēs ad maius malum sōlum dūxērunt.

Narration

The Donkey and the Dog (Asinus et Canis)
Write a narration of the story below. Retell the story using as much detail as possible. After writing the retelling of the myth, include the moral. Use the prompts below to start your writing.
The story goes. . . .
The moral is . . .

Vocabulary Review

Fill in the Latin or English word in the blank.

Avibus- _____

Donkey- _____

 Vident- _____

Omnia - _____

Feles- _____

Canī (canis) - _____

Ignore - _____

Nemo - _____

Mutat - _____

Consilium - _____

Turbas - _____

Agere - _____

Servi - _____

Answer Key
for
Vocabulary Review

Vocabulary Review

Match the Latin word with the English meaning.

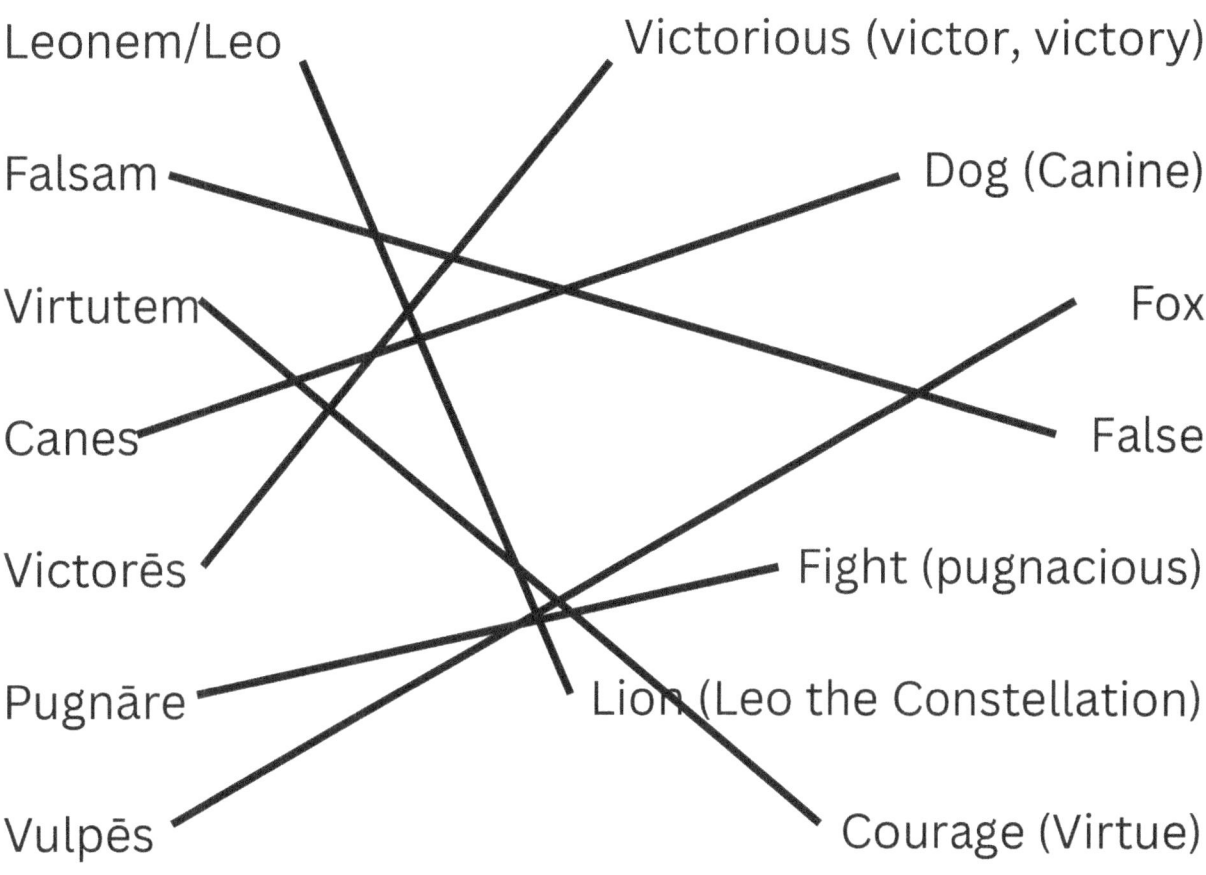

Leonem/Leo

Falsam

Virtutem

Canes

Victorēs

Pugnāre

Vulpēs

Victorious (victor, victory)

Dog (Canine)

Fox

False

Fight (pugnacious)

Lion (Leo the Constellation)

Courage (Virtue)

Vocabulary Review

Fill in the blank with the correct English meaning

Leo - Lion

Mūris - Mouse

Parvum - Small, little

Rēx (rēg) - King

Amīcus - Friend

Multis -Many (multiple)

Animalia –Animal, creature

Vēnātōrēs – Hunters

Audit - Hear

Vocabulary Review

Match the Latin word with the English meaning.

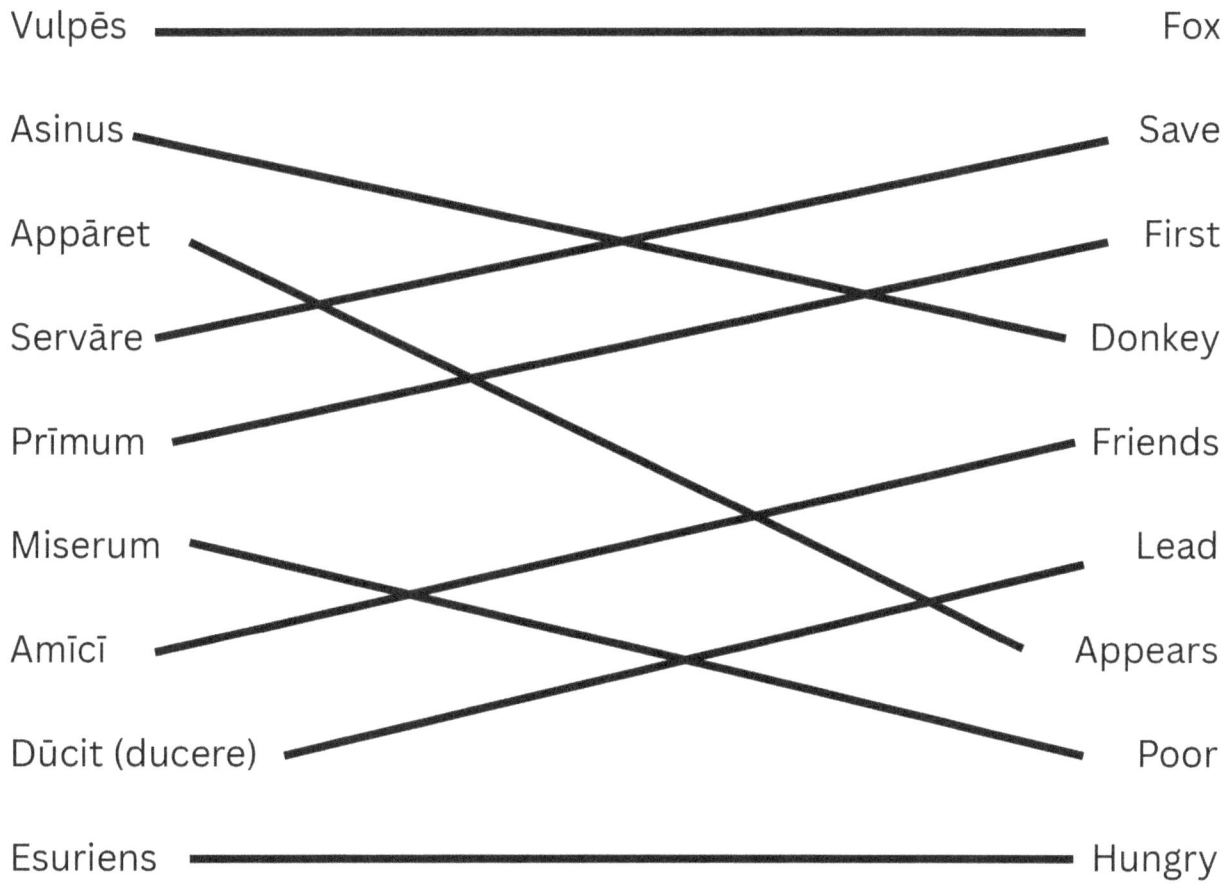

Vulpēs — Fox

Asinus — Save

Appāret — First

Servāre — Donkey

Prīmum — Friends

Miserum — Lead

Amīcī — Appears

Dūcit (ducere) — Poor

Esuriens — Hungry

Vocabulary Review

Look at the pictures and write the words in the correct place

Leo	Pulcher	Asinus	Vulpis
Vetus	Aper	Ineptus	Dormis
Fortis	Taurus	Timet	Liberat

Fortis

Aper

Cōnsūmere

Timēbant

Leo

Vulpis

Taurus

Amīcī

Asinus

Pulcher

Rēx

Vetus

Vocabulary Review

```
W  W  C  U  N  T  T  S  N  Q  N  V  E  G  G  I  W
V  Z  F  R  B  E  E  K  P  Y  G  R  P  N  N  H  A
E  Z  U  L  T  Q  D  D  J  D  S  P  R  I  I  O  J
L  M  E  T  N  T  I  C  I  P  S  N  I  R  V  N  Y
F  V  V  H  G  S  V  Q  E  V  W  Y  W  A  O  E  Y
P  E  K  M  T  Y  P  G  D  C  T  B  W  C  L  S  O
D  U  A  R  F  L  J  O  G  N  I  Z  A  M  A  T  S
X  D  O  D  P  H  P  R  E  M  O  V  E  T  L  F  E
A  N  E  G  V  A  C  I  O  U  S  F  I  G  U  U  N
G  S  Y  V  W  E  T  Q  V  T  P  N  N  G  F  T  T
Q  W  I  G  O  A  N  K  A  O  I  I  L  T  T  I  I
Z  A  E  N  P  L  V  I  O  M  N  E  S  A  H  D  T
F  J  F  L  U  K  E  R  E  S  A  X  O  J  G  A  U
J  C  I  S  H  S  Q  M  U  N  M  B  Z  R  U  V  M
H  V  Y  W  W  S  S  R  X  N  T  O  V  U  O  E  G
V  R  B  P  E  D  E  M  R  A  R  E  U  H  W  X
E  M  U  I  L  I  S  N  O  C  G  G  M  Y  T  H  V
```

ĪNSPICIT	ADVENIENTEM	PEDEM
ĒVĀDIT	SPINAM	ASINUS
CŌNSILIUM	SENTIT	VIDET
LUPUS		

Vocabulary Review

Match the Latin word with the English meaning.

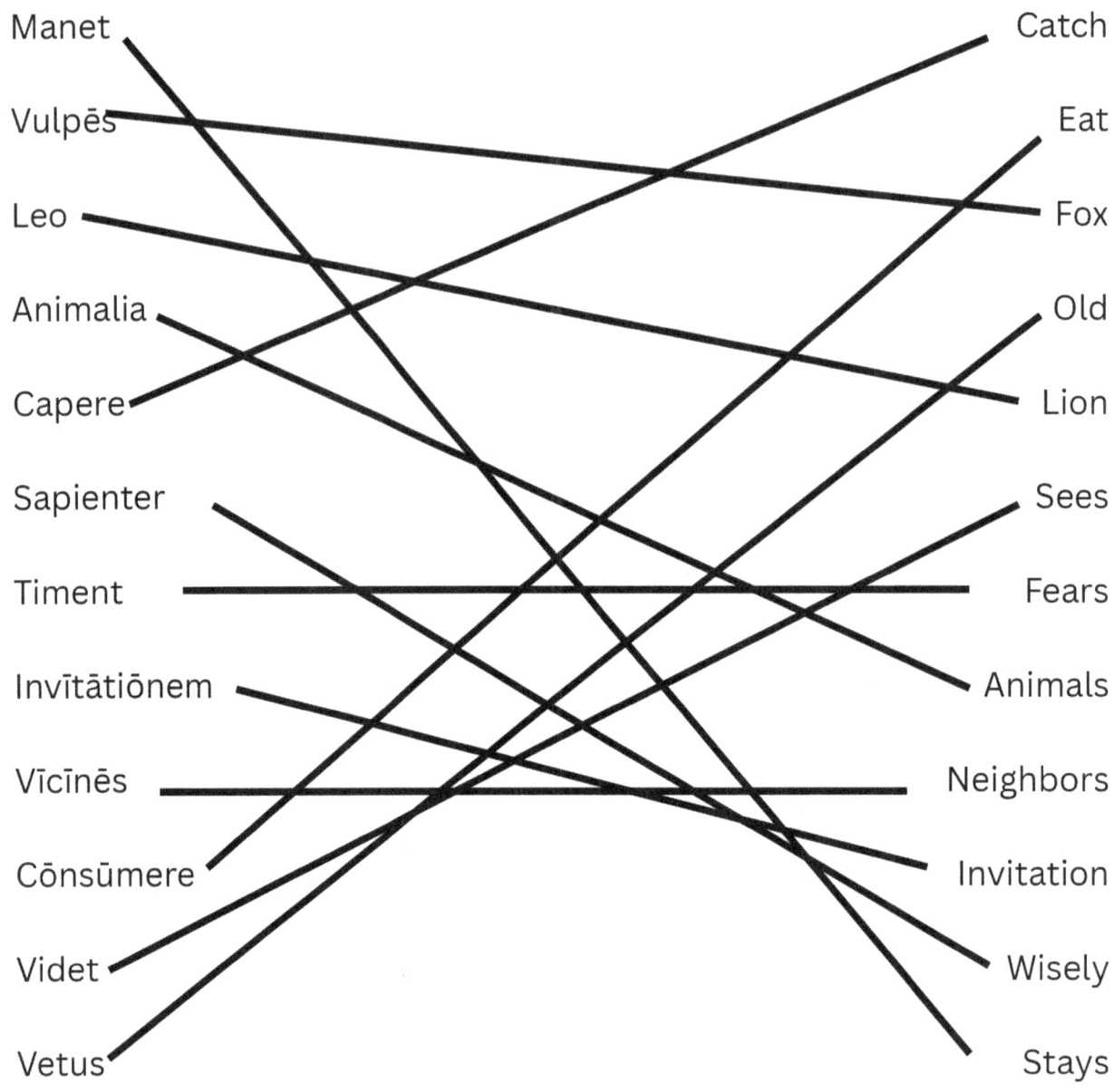

Manet

Vulpēs

Leo

Animalia

Capere

Sapienter

Timent

Invītātiōnem

Vīcīnēs

Cōnsūmere

Videt

Vetus

Catch

Eat

Fox

Old

Lion

Sees

Fears

Animals

Neighbors

Invitation

Wisely

Stays

Vocabulary Review

Match the Latin word with the English meaning.

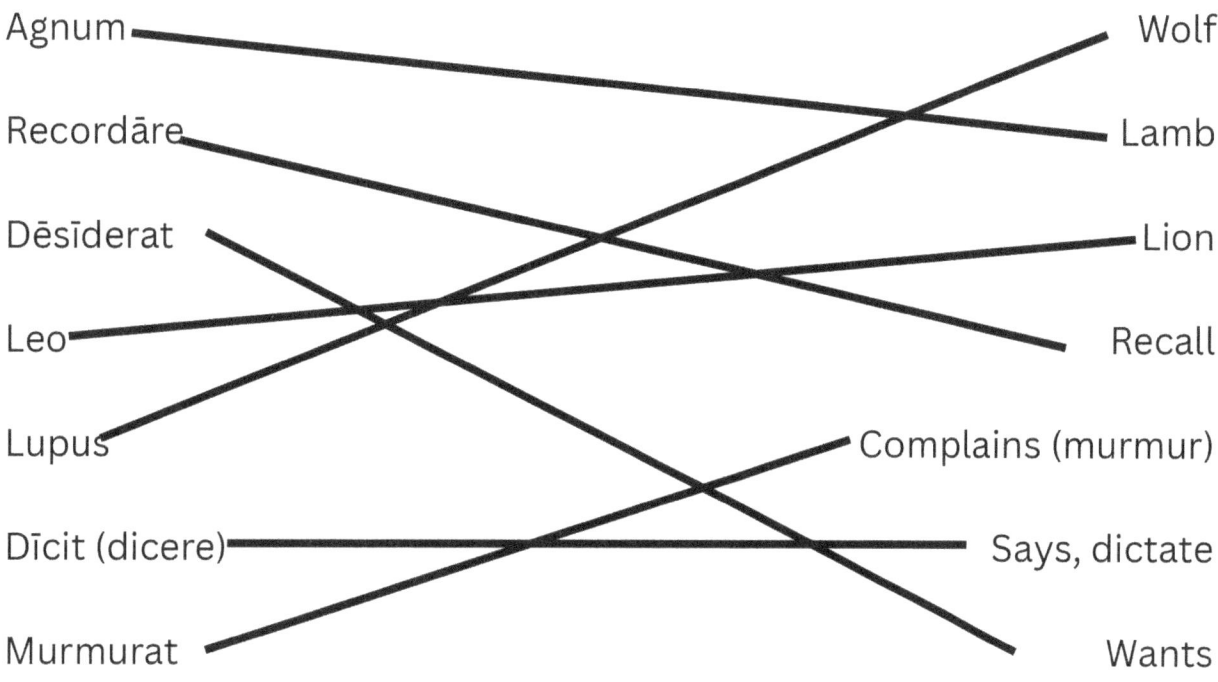

Agnum	Wolf
Recordāre	Lamb
Dēsīderat	Lion
Leo	Recall
Lupus	Complains (murmur)
Dīcit (dicere)	Says, dictate
Murmurat	Wants

Vocabulary Review

Fill in the English definition in the blank.

Videt - sees, video

Grandem - grand

Convenit - meets

Canis - dog

Putat - thinks

Invitat –invite

Lupus –wolf

Libertas - liberty

Audit - hears

Vital - life

Laudat - Praises

Vocabulary Review

Look at the pictures and write the words in the correct place

Vulpis	Arborem	Bibe	Lupus
Aquam	Caprum	Salit	Leonem
Faciem	Canis	Puteum	Catēnā

Arborem Faciem Canis

Salit Caprum Catēnā

Bibe Vulpis Leonem

Aquam Lupus Puteum

Vocabulary Review

Fill in the Latin word for the definition in the blank.

Fox Vulpes

Bear -Ursus

Hungry - Esurientes

Tired - Fessissimi

Want- Dēsīderant

Collapse - Collābuntur

Lion – Leo

Watch/See – Spectate

Takes - Capit

Kid/ Young Goat - Haedum

Fight - Pungent

Vocabulary Review

Across

1. Wolf

3. Safe

7. Want

9. Rock

Down

2. Goat

4. Spies, catches sight of

5. Bear

6. Grass, plants

Vocabulary Review

Match the Latin word with the English meaning.

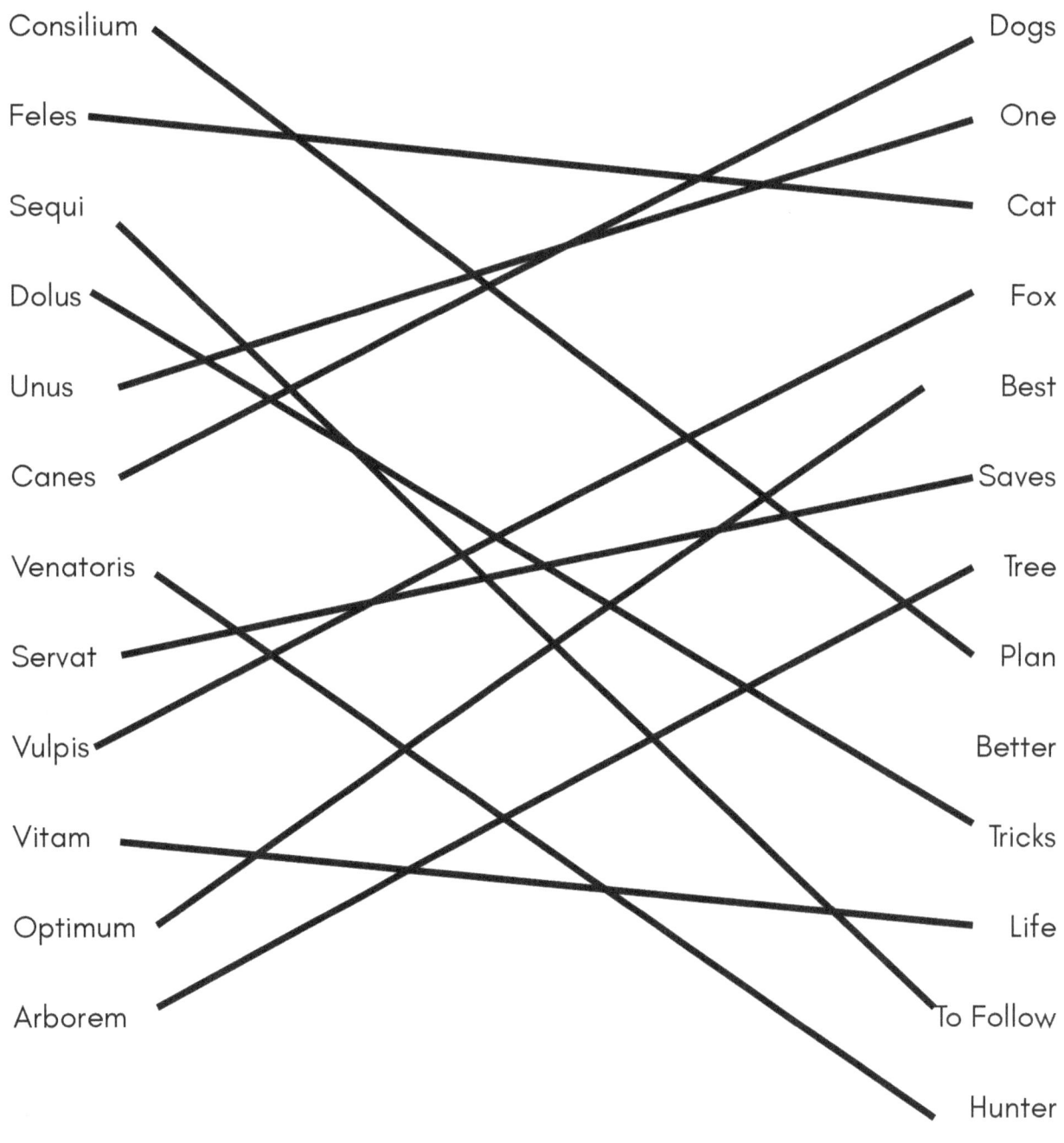

Consilium   Dogs

Feles   One

Sequi   Cat

Dolus   Fox

Unus   Best

Canes   Saves

Venatoris   Tree

Servat   Plan

Vulpis   Better

Vitam   Tricks

Optimum   Life

Arborem   To Follow

     Hunter

Vocabulary Review

Fill in the Latin or English word in the blank.

All – Omnia

Lion – Leoni

Turns – Vertit

Place – Loco

Donkey – Asinus

Animals – Animalia

Way, Path – Viam

Great – Magno

Stoops, Goes down – Descendit

Vocabulary Review

Fill in the Latin or English word in the blank.

Avibus- birds

Donkey- Asinus

Vident- See

Omnia - All

Feles- Cat

Canī (canis) - Dog

Ignore - Neglegite

Nemo - no one

Mutat - changes

Consilium - Plan

Turbas - mess

Agere - Act

Servi - Servants